Motocross
RACING

By Alex Monnig

SportsZone

An Imprint of Abdo Publishing
www.abdopublishing.com

www.abdopublishing.com

Published by Abdo Publishing, a division of ABDO, PO Box 398166, Minneapolis, Minnesota 55439. Copyright © 2015 by Abdo Consulting Group, Inc. International copyrights reserved in all countries. No part of this book may be reproduced in any form without written permission from the publisher. SportsZone™ is a trademark and logo of Abdo Publishing.

Printed in the United States of America, North Mankato, Minnesota
032014
092014

Cover Photo: Jody Warner/AP Images
Interior Photos: Jody Warner/AP Images, 1; Larry Lawrence/AP Images, 4–5, 10; Lubos Pavlicek/AP Images, 7; Shutterstock Images, 8, 20–21, 23, 25, 26, 28–29, 30–31, 36; AP Images, 12–13, 15, 17; Kelly Jordan/AP Images, 19; Norm Dettlaff/AP Images, 33; Greg Wood/Newscom, 35; Phil Sandlin/AP Images, 38–39; David Tucker/Daytona Beach News-Journal/AP Images/AP Images, 41; American Honda Racing/AP Images, 42; Phil Sandlin/AP Images, 45

Editor: Patrick Donnelly
Series Designer: Craig Hinton

Library of Congress Control Number: 2014932862

Cataloging-in-Publication Data
Monnig, Alex.
 Motocross racing / Alex Monnig.
  p. cm. -- (Inside the speedway)
Includes bibliographical references and index.
ISBN 978-1-62403-405-3
1. Motocross--Juvenile literature. 2. Motorcycle racing--Juvenile literature. I. Title.
796.7--dc23

2014932862

TABLE OF CONTENTS

chapter 1

THE DIRT ON MOTOCROSS

Ricky Carmichael was at the Spring Creek Motocross Park in Millville, Minnesota, in 2006. Fans had long known he was one of the best motocross racers of all time. On this day, Carmichael showed just how far ahead of the pack he was.

Racers headed to the starting line to prepare for the race. Then the skies opened. Rain poured onto the course. The track became a messy pit of hills and curves.

Ricky Carmichael races to victory at the Red Bud Track–n-Trail in 2005.

But the race went on. Carmichael burst from the gates with a holeshot. That means he took the lead before the first turn on the track. Mud flew from spinning tires. Other riders slid and slipped all over the track. They were covered head to toe in slop.

"There's guys going backwards on the track, trying to get runs up the hill," Carmichael said. "Next thing I know I'm lapping some pretty good guys."

He made his way around the track. He handled the steep hills and tight turns. Finally, he crossed the finish line. No other riders were close. But even Carmichael was unaware just how impressive his win was.

"When I got to the podium," he said, "they were like, 'Dude, you lapped second place!'"

Carmichael had passed the entire field. And the field had some top riders. Among them were stars such as Chad Reed

Freestyle motocross riders perform amazing tricks in midair to earn points.

and James "Bubba" Stewart. Carmichael is nicknamed the GOAT. That is short for Greatest of All Time. He showed why that day.

Motocross is an exciting sport. It involves high-speed motorcycle racing on a winding mud track. Riders have to deal with tricky obstacles. These obstacles might be steep hills or tight turns. Supercross is motocross held in large arenas.

It is perhaps the most popular form of motocross. The jumps in supercross are big. They send riders flying high into the air.

Another form of the sport is freestyle motocross. It was born from supercross. Freestyle motocross riders get even higher in the air. They fly off jumps and do tricks. The tricks involve flips and turns while the rider is still high in the air. Then judges score the riders. The rider with the highest score wins.

The best motocross racers join racing series. A series includes a number of races held all over the world. The riders earn points based on how they finish in the races. The American Motorcyclist Association (AMA) Motocross Championship is one of the biggest series. It takes place in

The GOAT

Ricky Carmichael was a professional rider from 1996 to 2006. He won 150 races. Carmichael also was named the AMA Pro Racing Athlete of the Year five times. That may not have been his most impressive feat, though. Carmichael swept every race in the AMA Motocross Championship series in three different years. No wonder people think he is the best rider ever.

the United States. The Motocross World Championship series has races all over the world. The Federation of International Motorcycle Racing (FIM) organizes this series. The FIM is a world governing body for the sport. One of the most famous freestyle events is at the X Games.

All of the racing series have similarities. Riders compete for different teams. These teams provide the riders with money and support. Teams also provide riders top-of-the-line racing gear. Big companies such as Honda and Suzuki manufacture bikes. Some of these companies also sponsor the racing teams. That means they provide money and equipment to the teams. There are different divisions of racing. The divisions are based on how powerful the motorcycle engines are.

Motocross is a hit all over the world. It has high-flying action. It has high speeds. It has fun, challenging courses. These factors have made it one of the most popular competitions on the planet.

chapter 2

MAKING MOTOCROSS

Every year more and more fans around the world turn out for motocross competitions. The sport got its start in England and France in the 1920s. Some motorcycle companies in England wanted to show off the power of their motorcycles in long outdoor races. There were different kinds of races through fields and forests. Races could last as long as six days.

Motocross riders race on a course in Czechoslovakia in 1965.

One form of racing was called scrambling. Racers started at different parts of the course at different times. They raced across hills and terrain. The challenging course allowed riders to catch up to each other. That meant the riders battled head to head.

The Southern Scott Scramble was held in England on March 29, 1924. Most historians say that race was the beginning of motocross.

The French took the scrambling idea and rode with it. They made the sport more exciting for the common fan. They shortened the courses. They also added extra jumps. The changes made the races more action-packed. The French also changed the name of the sport. They shortened the terms "motorcycle" and "cross-country." That created the new term "moto-cross."

Motocross racers battle on a course at Daytona International Speedway in 1974.

It took a while for motocross to take off in the United States. Official rules were created in the late 1950s. But the sport did not really become a hit for another 10 years.

Edison Dye was an American motorcycle enthusiast. He went to Europe in 1960 and opened a motorcycle touring company. During his stay in Europe, he fell in love with motocross. In the late 1960s, he had a plan. Dye arranged for some of the top European riders to compete in the United States.

Foreign riders dominated the races. The Europeans flew effortlessly around the track. Their flair was exciting. It was different from early US races. But the fans were hooked. The events influenced a new generation of motocrossers to hop on bikes.

That exciting style was taken to new heights in supercross. Concert promoter Mike Goodwin is credited with creating supercross. He staged the first event in 1972 at the Los Angeles Coliseum. The Superbowl of Motocross brought even more fans to the sport.

That year was a big one for the sport. Biker Gary Jones won an international series. He became the first American to

The Superbowl of Motocross, shown in 1978 in Los Angeles, triggered the explosion of supercross.

do so. The AMA also started its motocross championships in the United States that year. US riders began to catch up to the Europeans who had helped introduce them to the sport. Millions of motorcycles were sold in the 1970s.

The races started attracting more competitors and fans. Different forms of the sport began to grow. In the 1990s, rider Jeremy McGrath started doing stunts off big jumps in races. That led to the creation of freestyle motocross.

chapter 3

BIG BAD BIKES

Motocross has gotten more competitive since its creation. Much of this has to do with the riders' improved skills. But the motorcycles also have improved. They can go faster and fly higher in the air.

Motorcycles are often classified in two primary ways. One way is by brand. Many companies make motorcycles. Honda and Suzuki make some of the most popular

Motocross has grown in popularity as the bikes have become more powerful.

motorcycles in motocross. These companies also make some of the best-selling cars in the world.

Motorcycles are also classified by engine power. That is determined by how much room is in the engine for the reactions that power the bikes. The unit of measurement for this area is the cubic centimeter (cc). More powerful engines have more cc. The AMA Motocross Championship has separate competitions based on engine class. They range from 125 to 500 cc.

Motocross bikes differ from commercial motorcycles. Motocross bikes are ridden on dirt. So they are built to handle the tough muddy terrain of indoor and outdoor courses. Dirt bike tires have special grooves and ridges. These features allow for better grip on slippery ground. They provide traction in the sloppy conditions. There are different types of tires for harder and softer tracks. Bikers always make sure to have valve caps. These caps cover the tiny stems where air enters

Team Time

Professional riders are often sponsored. That means a company supports them with money and equipment. Bike manufacturers are common sponsors. These companies often sponsor an entire team. In that case, every rider on that team uses the company's gear and motorcycles in races. It works out well for both parties. The riders get access to the best equipment. The companies get their goods shown off to the world.

the tires. The caps keep dirt from getting stuck in the tips of the stems, which can cause air to leak out.

The wheels are attached to the body by a sturdy, pronged piece of metal called a fork. Hardworking shock absorbers are in the fork. They are one of the most important motorcycle parts. Riders go over many bumps and land from impressive heights. Good shocks allow racers to stay in control. Riders can get back up to speed quickly after each bump and jump.

Riders speed up and slow down by twisting and pulling parts of the handlebars. There are separate brake levers for the front and rear wheels.

The riders sit on a seat on the motorcycle frame. The frames also are a little different than normal bikes. Namely, motocross vehicles have smaller frames. Riders sacrifice comfort for a lighter bike. The lighter weight allows for more speed and better control.

Motocross is a dangerous sport. Even the best riders can crash at any moment. That is why riders are covered in safety gear from head to toe. Helmets and goggles protect the head and eyes. Padding on the torso and arms protects the majority of the body. Finally, sturdy boots help riders handle the slop on the course. The boots allow riders to plant their feet into the ground if they need to restart.

Motorcycles have a lot of different parts. It takes a lot of practice and a lot of skill to be able to fly around the course with them.

MOTOCROSS Photo Diagram

1. **TIRES:** Made from highly durable rubber, these help grip the slippery surfaces as riders speed around the track.

2. **FORK:** This connects the wheels to the rest of the body of the bike and also contains shocks to help ensure a smoother ride.

3. **HELMET:** This protective gear covers the entire head. Goggles keep dirt out of the eyes of riders.

4. **HANDLEBARS:** Riders hang on to them when operating the bike. The handlebars also feature the instruments used to accelerate and brake.

5. **SEAT:** The seat helps absorb the beating the rider takes while tackling obstacles. It also helps riders avoid injury.

6. **PEGS:** Riders set their feet on these while on the bike. Pegs are especially helpful for when riders stand up on the bike and shift their weight.

7. **ENGINE:** What makes the motorcycle go. Engines can create more or less power depending on their size.

5

chapter 4

SUPER SKILLS

P rofessional motocross riders make the sport look easy. They roll up to the gate and calmly wait for the start of the race. Then they gun their engines and cruise around the course. But there is a lot more to excelling in the sport. Speed is important. But being able to control one's speed at the right time also is important. So is vision. Riders must be able to navigate around the tricky obstacles on the courses.

Riders line up for the start of a 2013 race.

Riders start races side by side. A good start is important. A rider who shoots out of the gate has a clear path. Those who start out slowly may get caught behind the pack. Reaction time is key to getting out in front. Champion Ricky Carmichael has a routine when he gets to the starting line. He says he only looks at the small gate in front of his tire. When the gate drops, he turns the throttle and takes off.

Again, it is not as easy as it looks. Accelerating too quickly can make the front wheel of the bike fly up. This is called a wheelie. Riders must lean forward to keep the bike under control.

Body control is one of the most important skills in all forms of motocross. Turns on the tracks are tight. Courses are filled with deep ruts. These ruts make turns even harder to handle. Riders keep their weight centered on the bike, and they lean on the motorcycle. They press the tires into the rut. Then the bikers accelerate at the right time to get back up to speed.

Fans love watching the riders go off huge jumps. But being in the air is actually a bad thing for motocross riders. The bikes only accelerate when they are touching the ground. Too much air time slows the rider down. That is where scrubbing comes in. It takes place as riders take off at the top of a jump. They turn their bikes almost parallel to the ground and whip the back wheel around. That "scrubs," or reduces, some of the speed to keep the riders from flying too high off the jump.

Nac Nac Attack

Jeremy McGrath dominated supercross during the 1990s. He was often so far ahead of his opponents that he had time to do tricks off jumps. His most famous trick is called a Nac Nac. In it he pulls one of his legs over his bike, like he is getting off of it. Then he returns the leg to its peg before landing. McGrath's tricks inspired the creation of freestyle motocross.

Riders can get back on the ground faster. There they can make up for the lost time in the air.

Perhaps the most obvious form of body control takes place in freestyle motocross. Riders are given points by judges based on the types of jumps and stunts they perform. In freestyle, the

riders fly dozens of feet into the air and perform all sorts of crazy twists and turns.

Over the years, tricks have gotten more and more intense. One trick is called the double grab. Riders grab the back of the bike's seat while the rest of their body flies behind the bike.

Riders need tremendous strength to keep their bikes upright and moving forward on the rough terrain of a motocross course.

Another trick is called the coffin. Riders lay down on the seat of the bike. Then they stick their feet out straight and hook them under the handlebars. Flips and full turns have also become key pieces in riders' bags of tricks.

All forms of motocross can be dangerous. It takes years of practice to get ready to compete. Freestylers practice tricks by going off ramps and landing in big pits filled with foam rubber.

Motocross drivers must also be strong. The bike does a lot of the work. But maneuvering the heavy bikes can be difficult. Riders need to be able to control their machines when turning and flying through the air. Most riders lift weights to stay in shape and build the strength necessary to control their bikes.

chapter 5

MOTOCROSS MASTERS

Motocross riders are naturally wild. After all, they are driving bikes at high speeds and flying through the air. Fans have had plenty of characters to cheer for over the years. As the sport has grown, so has the profile of the riders.

Bob "Hurricane" Hannah was one of the first and most successful riders. He did not grow up racing dirt bikes. But he made up for lost time. Hannah discovered his love

Bob "Hurricane" Hannah was one of the most dominant motocross riders of the 1970s and 1980s.

for racing at age 18. Within a year, he was racing in the AMA Championship events. Bike manufacturer Yamaha signed on to sponsor him as well.

Hurricane went on to destroy the competition for 15 years. Then he retired in 1989. What made Hannah such an exciting racer was his ability to compete in different classes. When he left the sport, he was one of only two men to win AMA championships in 125 cc and 250 cc motocross and in supercross. He was one of the first riders to successfully ride in both motocross and supercross championships. Hannah's 70 combined AMA wins were a record until 1999.

Jeremy McGrath broke Hannah's record. McGrath brought a new age of showmanship to motocross. He had a fun attitude and wild haircuts. That helped make the sport cool for a younger generation of riders in the 1990s. McGrath was even well known by people who did not follow dirt biking.

His feats on the track were even more outstanding. McGrath was supposed to spend the 1993 season learning

Jeremy McGrath wins another race in style at the 1996 Daytona 250 Supercross.

from teammate Jeff Stanton. Stanton was an AMA champion.
But at the Anaheim Supercross that year, McGrath passed
him. It was McGrath's first supercross race. There were many
more wins after that. McGrath won seven of the eight AMA

supercross titles between 1993 and 2000. That established him as one of the best supercross riders of all time. He retired with records of 72 AMA supercross victories and 89 total AMA wins.

But even McGrath was outdone by the GOAT, Ricky Carmichael, who is considered the best motocross rider of all time. Carmichael was named AMA Athlete of the Year a record five times in his 11-year career. And his total of 150 AMA victories is a record that might never be matched.

Now there is a new generation of exciting riders. One of them is Ashley Fiolek. She is deaf. But she has not let that slow her down. In 2008 Fiolek became the youngest Women's Motocross Association champion ever. She was 19 years old. Then she went on to win the 2009, 2011, and 2012 AMA women's championships. She also became the first female rider to be sponsored by the popular Honda Red Bull Racing team.

Motocross in all its forms continues to grow. The trailblazers set a great example for others to follow. It will take a long time for another rider to come along and challenge the success of bikers such as Hannah, McGrath, and Carmichael. But a new and exciting group of riders will keep trying. They will push the limits of themselves and their bikes to excite their fans.

Marty Tripes

Marty Tripes took up motocross after watching the European riders brought over by Edison Dye. Tripes earned 11 AMA national championships. He also won the 1972 Superbowl of Motocross. That event started supercross.

GLOSSARY

OBSTACLES
Hills, bumps, and turns that make it hard for riders to get around the course.

PEGS
Small rods that stick out of the side of the bike that riders plant their feet on while racing.

RUT
A groove in the ground either built into the course or caused by multiple bikes riding over the same part of a track.

SCRUBBING
Twisting a motorcycle in midair so it gets less air and lands quicker off a jump.

SERIES
A set of races in which riders compete throughout a season.

SHOCK
A piece of motorcycle equipment that absorbs the pressure and force of landing.

SHOWMANSHIP
Acting in an exciting and entertaining manner.

SPONSORED
When a company provides a rider with free racing gear, equipment, and other support.

TERRAIN
The land on which riders compete during races.

TRACTION
The grip that allows a tire to stay on the ground.

WHEELIE
When the front wheel rises off the ground so a bike is just riding on its back wheel.

FOR MORE INFORMATION

Further Readings

Fiolek, Ashley, and Caroline Ryder. *Kicking Up Dirt: A True Story of Determination, Deafness, and Daring*. New York: It Books, 2010.

LaPlante, Gary. *How to Ride Off-Road Motorcycles*. Minneapolis, MN: Motorbooks, 2012.

Madigan, Tom. *Hurricane!: The Bob Hannah Story*. Minneapolis, MN: Motorbooks, 2008.

Woods, Bob. *Motocross History*. St. Catharines, ON: Crabtree Publishing, 2008.

Websites

To learn more about Inside the Speedway, visit **booklinks.abdopublishing.com**. These links are routinely monitored and updated to provide the most current information available.

INDEX

About the Author

Alex Monnig is a freelance journalist from St. Louis, Missouri. He graduated with his master's degree from the University of Missouri in May 2010. During his career, he has spent time covering sporting events around the world, including the 2008 Olympic Games in China, 2011 Rugby World Cup in New Zealand, and the 2014 Olympic Games in Sochi, Russia.